Real Science-4-Kids

Level I

Laboratory Workbook

Dr. R. W. Keller

Cover design: David Keller
Opening page: David Keller, Rebecca Keller
Illustrations: Rebecca Keller

Copyright © 2004, 2005, 2007 Gravitas Publications, Inc.

Real Science-4-Kids: Physics Level I-Laboratory Workbook

ISBN 0-9749149-5-9

Published by Gravitas Publications, Inc.
P.O. Box 4790
Albuquerque, NM 87196-4790

GRAVITAS
PUBLICATIONS INC

Keeping a Laboratory Notebook

A laboratory notebook is essential for the experimental scientist. In this notebook, the results for all of the experiments are kept together with comments and any additional information. For this curriculum, you should record your experimental observations and conclusions directly on these pages, which are designated as the laboratory notebook just like real scientists.

The experimental section for each chapter is prewritten. The exact format of a notebook may vary, but all experiments written in a laboratory notebook have certain essential parts. For each experiment, a descriptive but short *Title* is written at the top of the page along with the *Date* the experiment is performed.   Below the title, an *Objective* and *Hypothesis* are written. The objective is a short statement that tells something about why you are doing the experiment, and the hypothesis tells what is the predicted outcome. Next, a *Materials List* is written. The materials should be gathered before the experiment is started. Following the materials list, the *Experiment* is written. The sequence of steps for the experiment is written beforehand, and any changes should be noted during the experiment. All of the details of the experiment are written in this section. All information that might be of some importance is included. For example, if you are to measure out 1 cup of water for an experiment, but you actually measured $1\frac{1}{4}$ cup, this should be recorded. It is sometimes hard to predict how small variations in an experiment will affect the outcome, but it is easier to track a problem if all of the information is recorded.

The next section is the *Results* section. Here you record your experimental observations. It is extremely important that you be honest about what is observed. For example, if the experimental instructions say that a solution will turn yellow but your solution turned blue record blue. You may have done the experiment incorrectly or you might have discovered a new and interesting result, but either way it is very important that your observations be honestly recorded.

Finally, the *Conclusions* should be written. Here you will explain what the observations may mean. You should try to write only *valid* conclusions. It is important to learn to think about what the data actually show and what cannot be concluded from the experiment.

Laboratory Safety

Most of these experiments use household items. Extra care should be taken while working with all chemicals in this series of experiments. The following are some general laboratory precautions that should be applied to the home laboratory:

Never put things in your mouth without explicit instructions to do so. This means that food items should not be eaten unless tasting or eating is part of the experiment.

Use safety glasses while using glass objects or strong chemicals such as bleach.

Wash hands before and after handling chemicals.

Use adult supervision while working with electricity and while conducting any step requiring a stove.

Contents

Experiment 1:   It's the law!   Date: _____

Objective: In this experiment we will use the scientific method to determine Newton's first law of motion.

Hypothesis:

Materials:

        tennis ball
        yarn or string (10 ft)
        paper clip
        marble

Experiment:

  Part I

1. Take the tennis ball outside and throw it as far as you can. Observe how the ball travels through the air. Sketch the path of the ball in the space below.

2. Now, take the string or yarn and attach it to the tennis ball using the paper clip. To do this, open the paper clip up on one side and slightly curve the end as follows:

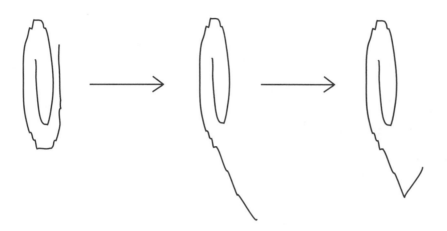

3. Put the extended curved end of the paper clip into the tennis ball by gently pushing and twisting.

4. Next, tie the string to the end of the paper clip.

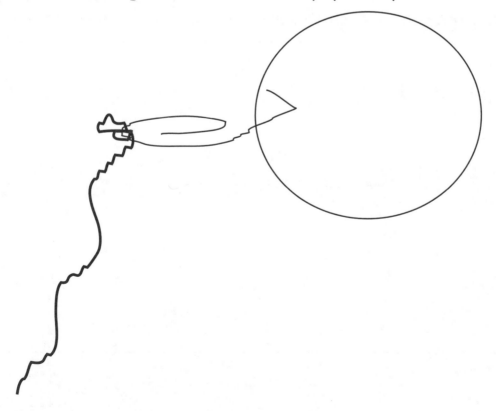

5. Holding onto one end of the string, throw the ball again into the air as far as you can. Note how the ball travels, and record what you see in the space below. Do this several times.

Part II

1. Take the marble and find a straight clear path on the floor or outdoors. Roll the marble on the floor and record how it travels. Note where and how it stops or changes direction. Do this several times and record your observations in the next box.

Conclusions:

● Review

Define the following:

physics

_____

_____

law

_____

_____

●

List the 5 steps of the scientific method

_____

_____

_____

_____

_____

●

NOTES:

_____

_____

_____

_____

_____

_____

_____

_____

_____

_____

_____

_____

_____

Experiment 2:   Fruit works?   Date: _____

Objective: _____

_____

Hypothesis: _____

_____

Materials:

    slinky
    paper clips(2)
    apple
    lemon or lime
    banana
    ruler
    balance or food scale

Experiment:

1. Try to decide, just by "weighing" each piece of fruit in your hands which piece will do the most work and which piece will do the least work on the spring.

2. State your prediction as the hypothesis.

3. Now, weigh each piece of fruit on the balance or food scale.

4. Record the weights on the next chart.

Fruit	Weight (oz. or g)

5. Next, take the paper clip and stretch one side out to make a small hook.

6. Place the hook in one of the pieces of fruit.

7. Hold the slinky up to the level of your chest and allow 10 to 15 coils to hang below. You will have to hold most of the slinky in your hand.

8. Measure the distance from the floor to the bottom of the slinky with the tape measure. Record your result below.

Distance from floor to slinky

9. Now place the piece of fruit that has the hook in it on the slinky and allow the slinky to be pulled out by the fruit.

10. Measure from the end of the slinky to the floor with the tape measure and record your results below.

11. Repeat with each piece of fruit. Record your results in the next chart.

Results:

Fruit	Distance from floor to slinky	Distance extended

11. Subtract the distance you recorded in step 8 from each of the distances you measured and recorded in the previous chart. This gives you the distance each piece of fruit has extended the slinky.

12. Calculate the work each piece of fruit has done. Record your answers in the next chart.

Fruit	Work

13. What would happen if you put two pieces of fruit on the slinky? Test your prediction and record your answer below.

(2)Fruit	Work

14. Make some conclusions about your results and record them in the conclusions section.

Conclusions:

_____

_____

_____

_____

_____

_____

_____

_____

_____

_____

_____

_____

_____

Review

Define the following terms:

force   _____
         _____

work   _____
         _____

energy _____
         _____

Circle the correct answer in each pair for the following question:

     Which object has the greater gravitational force:

         a banana or a bowling ball
         a car or a bicycle
         the moon or the earth
         the earth or the sun

Answer the following questions:

     Is a book sitting on a shelf doing work?   _____
     Is a bowling ball crashing into the pins doing work?   _____
     How much work is done if you lift a 3-lb box 2 feet?   _____
     How much work is done if you lift a 2-lb box 3 feet?   _____

List some forms of energy:

     _____   _____   _____

Challenge:

Do you think if we could get every person on the earth to jump all at once we could move the earth? Why or why not? Can you do a rough calculation?

NOTES:

Experiment 3:   Smashed banana   Date: _____

Objective: _____
_____

Hypothesis: _____
_____

Materials:

    stiff cardboard
    board (over 3 feet)
    straight pin or tack
    small scale or balance
    small to medium-sized toy car (1)
    one banana sliced
    10 - 20 Pennies

Experiment:

1. Read through the laboratory instructions and then write an objective and a hypothesis for this experiment.

2. Take a portion of the cardbord and make a backing to put the sliced bananas on. Attach a sliced piece of banana to the cardboard near the bottom.

3. Make a ramp with the board.   The end of the ramp should meet the sliced banana. Your setup should look like the next figure:

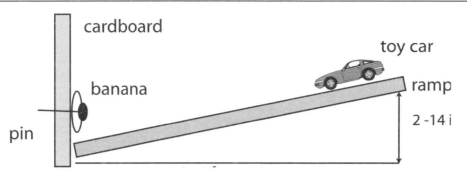

4. Weigh the toy car with the scale or balance. Record your result.

Weight of toy car (ounces or grams) =

5. Place the toy car on the ramp and elevate the ramp 2 inches. Allow the toy car to roll down the ramp and hit the banana. Record your results in the next chart.

6. Elevate the ramp another two inches. Now, the ramp should be 4 inches off the ground. Allow the toy car to roll down the ramp and hit the banana. Record your results in the chart below

7. Repeat with the ramp elevated 6 inches, 8 inches, 12 inches and 14 inches and record your results in the following chart.

Height (inches or centimeters)	Results (write your comments)
2 inches (4 centimeters)	
4 inches (8 centimeters)	
6 inches (12 centimeters)	
8 inches (16 centimeters)	
10 inches (20 centimeters)	
12 inches (24 centimeters)	
14 inches (28 centimeters)	

Answer the following questions:

1. What happened to the speed of the car as the ramp height increased? _____

2. At which ramp height did the banana smash? _____

8. Now add 10 pennies to the toy car. Weigh the toy car again and repeat rolling the toy car with the pennies down the ramp with the ramp elevated 2 inches, 4 inches, 6 inches, 8 inches, 12 inches, and 14 inches. Record your results.

Weight of toy car plus 10 pennies (ounces or grams) = _____

Distance (inches or centimeters)	Results (write your comments)
2 inches (4 centimeters)	
4 inches (8 centimeters)	
6 inches (12 centimeters)	
8 inches (16 centimeters)	
10 inches (20 centimeters)	
12 inches (24 centimeters)	
14 inches (28 centimeters)	

Answer the following questions:

1. At which ramp height did the banana smash? _____

2. Did the banana smash at the same height for the light car and the heavy car? _____

3. If "no" to question 3, which one was higher?

Using the equation,

gravitational potential energy = weight x height

Calculate the GPE for the height that smashes the banana for the toy car with and without the 10 pennies. Record your answers below.

GPE for car without pennies _____

GPE for car with pennies _____

Is the GPE the same [or close to the same] for both cars?_____

Conclusions:
_____
_____
_____
_____
_____
_____

● Review

Define the following terms:

potential energy _____

gravitational potential energy _____

chemical potential energy _____

kinetic energy _____

● Fill in the blanks for the following:

1 foot = _____ inches

1 yard = _____ feet

1 mile = _____ yards

1 meter = _____ centimeters

1 centimeter = _____ millimeters

1 gram = _____ kilogram

●

NOTES:

Experiment 4:   Moving marbles   Date: _____

Objective: _____

_____

Hypothesis: _____

_____

Materials:

    several glass marbles of different sizes
    steel marbles of different sizes
    cardboard (tube 2-3 ft. long)
    scissors
    black marking pen
    ruler
    two stop watches
    letter scale or balance

Experiment:

1. Using the letter scale or balance, weigh each of the marbles, both glass and steel. Label the marbles with numbers or letters or note their colors so that you can note what each marble weighs. Record your results in part "A."

2. Take the cardboard tube and cut it in half lengthwise to make a trough. Mark the middle of the tube with the black marking pen.

3. Measure one foot in either direction of the middle mark and make two more marks, one on each side.

4. The cardboard tube should now have three marks: one in the middle and two on each side one foot from the middle. The tube will be used as a track for the marbles.

5. Take the marbles and, one by one, roll them down the tube. Notice how each one rolls. Describe how they roll (do they roll straight? Are they easy to push off with your thumb? Do they pass the marks?) in Results, part "B."

6. Now place a glass marble on the center mark of the tube.

7. Roll a glass marble of the same size toward the marble in the center. Watch the two marbles as they collide. Record your results in Results, part "C."

8. Repeat steps 6 and 7 with different-sized marbles. Record your results in part "D." [For example, try rolling a heavy marble towards a light marble and a light marble towards a heavy marble.]

Results:

A.

Marble	Weight

B.

_____

_____

_____

_____

C.

_____

_____

_____

_____

D.

_____

_____

_____

_____

_____

_____

_____

_____

_____

_____

_____

Conclusions:

_____

_____

_____

_____

_____

_____

_____

_____

_____

_____

_____

_____

_____

Review

Define the following terms:

inertia

_____

_____

mass

_____

_____

momentum

_____

_____

friction

_____

_____

Write the equation for momentum:

Which has more mass: a bowling ball or a green pea? (circle one)

What has more momentum: a rolling bowling ball or a bowling ball shot from a cannon? (circle one)

NOTES:

Experiment 5:   Power pennies   Date: _____

Objective: _____

_____

Hypothesis: _____

_____

Materials:

        10-20 copper pennies
        paper towels
        aluminum foil
        salt water (2-3 T. salt per cup)
        voltmeter
        plastic-coated copper wire 4"-6" long
        strong tape (duct tape)

Experiment:

1. Cut out several penny-sized circles from the aluminum foil and paper towel.

2. Soak the paper-towel circles in salt water.

3. Strip off the end of one of the pieces of wire. Tape the exposed metal to a penny.

4. Strip off the end of another piece of wire. Tape the exposed metal to a piece of aluminum foil.

5. Putting the aluminum foil with the wire on the bottom, place one of the wet paper towel circles on the aluminum foil. Place the penny with the taped wire on top. It should look like this:

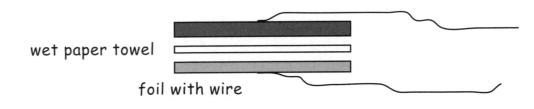

penny with wire

wet paper towel

foil with wire

6. Take the wires and connect them to the leads of the voltmeter. Switch the volt-meter to "voltage" and record the number. This is the amount of voltage the single-layer battery produces.

7. Add another "cell" to the battery and record the voltage. (A cell is a penny layer, a foil layer, and a paper layer.) It now has two cells. The battery should look like the following:

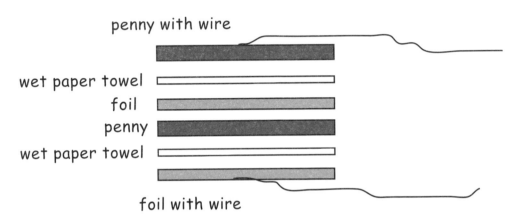

8. Continue adding cells of foil, wet paper towel, and pennies and record the voltage for each newly added cell.

Results:

Cell	Voltage
1	
2	
3	
4	
5	

Plot your data. Make a graph with "voltage" on the x-axis and "Number of Cells" on the y-axis.

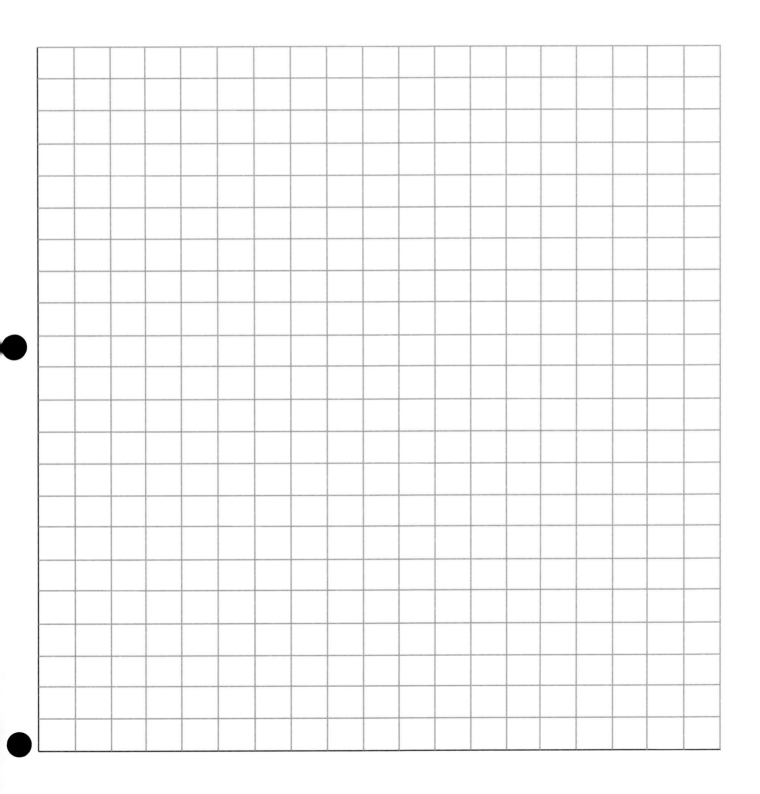

Discuss your data:

_____

_____

_____

_____

_____

_____

_____

_____

_____

_____

_____

_____

Conclusions:

_____

_____

_____

_____

_____

_____

_____

_____

_____

Review

Answer the following questions:

1. What is chemical energy?

_____

2. Give two foods that have "food energy" (carboydrates).

_____

_____

3. Give two examples of energy we use for fuel.

_____

_____

4. Who made the first battery?

_____

5. Draw a diagram of a voltaic battery.

NOTES:

Experiment 6:   Charge it!   Date: _____

Objective:

_____

_____

Hypothesis:

_____

_____

Materials:

       small glass jar
       aluminum foil
       paper clip
       strong tape (duct tape)
       plastic or rubber rod
       balloon
       silk fabric

Experiment:

A. Building an *electroscope* (an instrument that detects electric charge)

1. Cut two thin strips of aluminum foil of equal length (about 1.0" long).

2. Poke a small hole in the center of the lid of the glass jar.

3. Open one end of the paper clip to make a small hook.

4. Place the straight piece of the hook through the small hole in the glass jar lid and secure the paper clip to the lid with strong tape. Leave the end exposed.

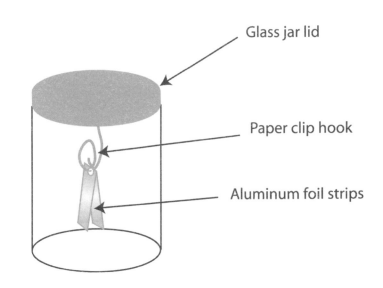

Glass jar lid

Paper clip hook

Aluminum foil strips

5. Hang the two strips of aluminum foil from the hook and place it inside the jar.

6. You now have an electroscope.

7. Take the plastic or rubber rod and rub it with the silk fabric, or take the balloon and rub it in your hair or on the cat.

8. Gently touch the balloon or plastic or rubber rod onto the paper clip that is sticking out from the glass lid.

9. Observe the two pieces of aluminum foil and record your results.

Results:

_____

_____

_____

_____

_____

_____

_____

_____

_____

_____

_____

_____

_____

_____

Conclusions:

_____

Review

Define the following terms:

dry cell   _____

electric charge   _____

electrical force   _____

Circle the correct word to complete the statement:

Like charges (repel or attract) each other.

Unlike charges (repel or attract) each other.

List the parts of an atom and whether or not they are charged:

_____

_____

_____

Experiment 7:   Let it flow   Date: _____

Objective: _____

_____

Hypothesis: _____

_____

Materials:

insulated electrical wire
12 V battery
some insulating materials (e.g. foam, plastic, cloth)
small light bulb
electrical tape
several small resistors

Experiment:

1. Cut the wire into two foot-long pieces. Carefully shave off the ends of the plastic insulation to expose the metal. Leave about 1/4 to 1/2 inch of expose metal on each end.

2. Tape one end of one wire to the (+) terminal of the battery. Tape one end of the other wire to the (-) terminal of the battery.

3. Tape the other ends of the two wires to the light bulb. One wire should be taped to the bottom of the bulb, and the other one should be taped to the metal side of the bulb.

4. Record your results.

5. Now place a piece of foam or plastic in between the wire and the bulb.

5. Record your results.

6. Remove one end of the wire from the battery and gently touch it with your finger to see if it is warm.

7. Record your results.

8. Place a resistor between the light bulb and the battery on one wire. Observe any difference in the intensity of the lightbulb. Record your results in the chart. Repeat with two or more resistors.

Results:

	wire only	wire + resistor(s)	wire + insulator
light bulb intensity			
temperature of wire			

Answer the following questions about your experiment:

1. What happened when you connected the battery to the light bulb?
   _____
   _____

2. What happened when you put a piece of foam or plastic between the wire and the bulb?
   _____
   _____

3. What happened when you put one or more resistors between the light bulb and the battery?
   _____
   _____

4. What did the wire feel like to your fingers (with the wire only, with the resistors, and with the insulator)?
   _____
   _____

Conclusions:

_____

_____

_____

_____

_____

_____

_____

_____

_____

_____

_____

_____

_____

_____

_____

_____

_____

Review

Define the following:

static electricity _____

_____

electric current _____

_____

voltage _____

_____

resistance _____

_____

conductor _____

_____

insulator _____

_____

heat _____

_____

Experiment 8:   Wrap it up!   Date: _____

● Objective: _____

_____

Hypothesis: _____

_____

Materials:

        metal rod
        electrical wire
        paper clips (10-20)
        12 V battery
        electrical tape

● Experiment:

1. Cut the metal wire so that it is one to two feet long.

2. Trim the ends of the wire so that there is 1/4 inch exposed metal.

3. Tape one end of the wire to the (+) terminal of the battery.

4. Tape the other end of the wire to the (-) terminal of the battery.

5. Take the metal rod and touch it to the paper clips. Record your results.

6. Coil the wire around the metal rod. The wire must remain hooked to the battery.

7. Touch the metal rod to the paper clips. Count the coils and record your results.

8. Wrap another 1 to 5 coils around the metal rod.

9. Touch the end of the metal rod to the paper clips. Record how many paper clips can be picked up.

10. Continue adding coils to the metal rod and counting the number of paper clips that can be picked up.

11. Record your results.

Results:

number of coils	number of paper clips

Graph your results below:

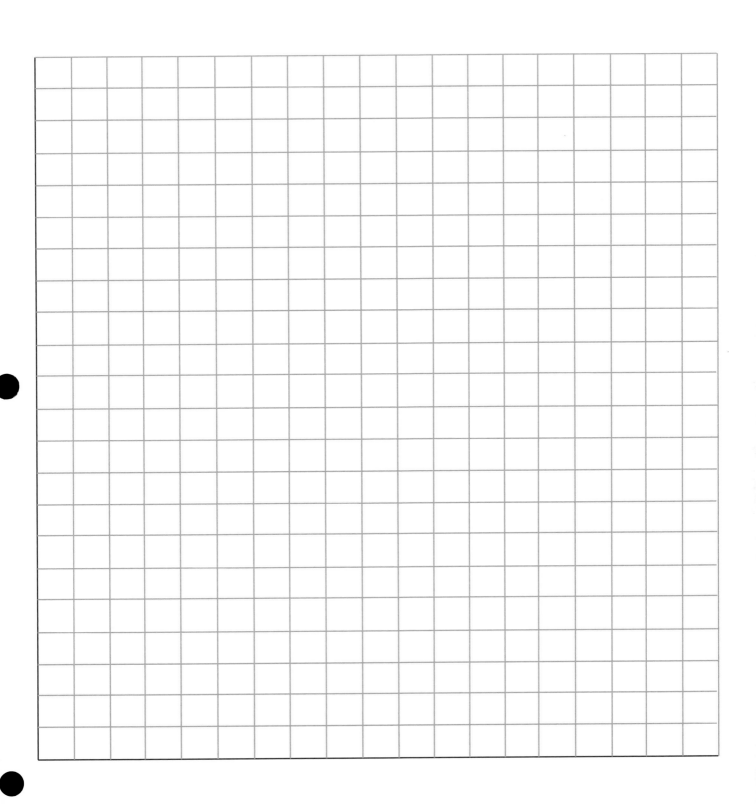

Conclusions:

_____

_____

_____

_____

_____

_____

_____

_____

_____

_____

_____

_____

_____

_____

Review

Answer the following questions:

1. What makes materials magnetic? _____

2. Why are some materials magnetic and others not? _____

   _____

3. What are poles? _____

   _____

4. Opposite poles attract or repel. (Circle the correct word.)

5. Like poles attract or repel. (Circle the correct word.)

6. What happens if an electric current flows around a metal rod?

   _____

7. What happens if a magnetic rod is pushed and pulled through a wire coil?

   _____

Draw a magnetic field.

NOTES:

Experiment 9 :   Bending light and circle sounds   Date: _____

Objective: _____
_____

Hypothesis: _____
_____

Materials:

two prisms (glass or plastic)
flashlight
metal can open at both ends
aluminum foil
rubber band
laser pointer
long wooden craft stick
colored pencils
stronge tape (such as duct tape)

Experiment:

Part I: Bending light

1. Take one prism and shine the flashlight through it at the 90° bend.
   (See illustration.) Record your results.

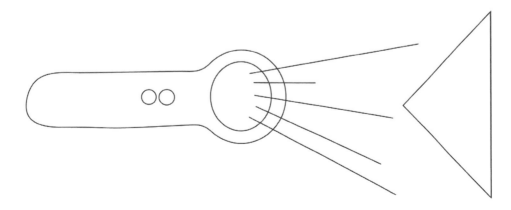

2. Now take the prism and shine sunlight through it from the same direction. Record your results.

3. Take the second prism and place it directly in front of the first one, laying it flat on one of the short edges. Using the flashlight, shine

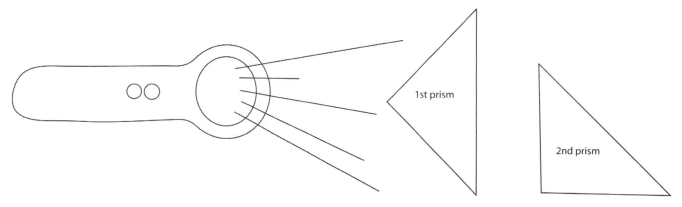

1st prism

2nd prism

light through the two prisms together. (See illustration.)

Results:
Part I

_____

1. What happens when you shine a flashlight through the prism?

_____

_____

2. What happens when you put the prism in sunlight?

_____

Draw what you see.

Part II: Circle sounds

Assemble a "sound scope" in the following way:

1. Take the metal can and make sure it is completely open on both ends.
2. Place a piece of aluminum foil over one end of the can and secure it with a rubber band. Be careful not to wrinkle the foil; try to keep it smooth.
3. Fix the craft stick to the metal can with strong tape.
4. Place the laser pointer with the light facing the foil on the craft stick. It should look like the setup in the next diagram.

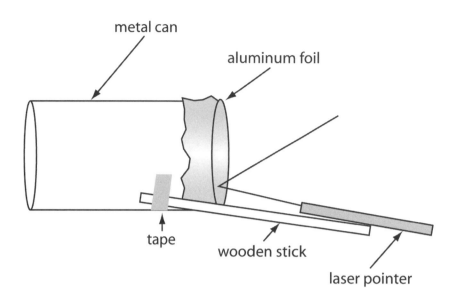

5. Turn on the laser pointer. (Be careful not to point the laser directly into the eyes!) Observe the reflection on a wall or white board.

6. Holding the can to your mouth, speak into it and watch what happens to the reflected laser light. Record your results.

7. Continue to speak or sing into the can, recording as many different shapes as you see.

Draw the shapes you see:

Review

Define the following terms:

electromagnetic wave _____

_____

wavelength _____

_____

amplitude _____

_____

electromagnetic spectrum _____

_____

visible light _____

_____

pitch _____

_____

frequency _____

_____

Are radio waves sound? _____

_____

Experiment 10:   On your own   Date: _____

You design this experiment. The goal is to convert as many forms of energy as you can into other forms of energy.

For example,

A scenario can be designed so that energy is used to put out a fire. A marble is rolled down a ramp and bumps into a domino with a small cap of baking soda on top of it. A chemical reaction is started when the baking soda falls into the vinegar, which produces carbond dioxide gas that puts out the fire. In this case the rolling marble has kinetic energy which is used to convert gravitational potential energy into kinetic energy (the falling baking soda), which then starts a chemical reaction.

Using Energy to Put Out a Fire

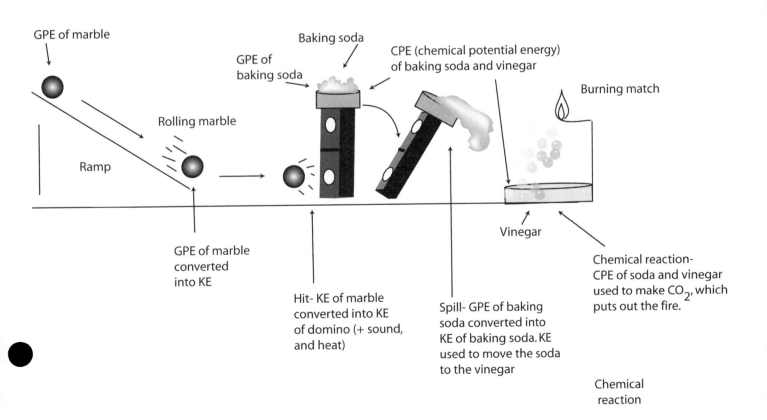

GPE of marble

Baking soda

GPE of baking soda

CPE (chemical potential energy) of baking soda and vinegar

Burning match

Rolling marble

Ramp

GPE of marble converted into KE

GPE of marble converted into KE

Hit- KE of marble converted into KE of domino (+ sound, and heat)

Spill- GPE of baking soda converted into KE of baking soda. KE used to move the soda to the vinegar

Vinegar

Chemical reaction- CPE of soda and vinegar used to make CO_2, which puts out the fire.

Chemical reaction

Use the following guide to design your experiment:

1. Write down all the different forms of energy you can think of.

   kinetic energy   _____

   _____   _____

   _____   _____

   _____   _____

2. Write down how these forms of energy can be represented.

   kinetic energy

        rolling marble   *moving toy car*   *moving ball*

   _____

            _____   _____   _____

   _____

            _____   _____   _____

   _____

            _____   _____   _____

   _____

            _____   _____   _____

3. Write down ways to connect two or more of these forms of energy, and explain how one form will be converted into another.

moving toy car bumps into marble and starts it rolling

4. Design an experiment to convert one form of energy into another. Give your experiment a title and write an objective and a hypothesis. Write down the materials you need and then set up a page to collect your results. See how many different forms of energy you can convert. Make careful observations and draw conclusions based on what you observe.

Experiment 10: _____ Date: _____

Objective: _____
_____

Hypothesis: _____
_____

Materials:

_____   _____   _____

_____   _____   _____

_____   _____   _____

Experiment:

_____

_____

_____

_____

_____

_____

_____

_____

_____

_____

_____

_____

_____

_____

_____

Results:

_____
_____
_____
_____
_____
_____
_____
_____
_____
_____
_____
_____
_____
_____
_____
_____
_____
_____

Conclusions:

_____
_____
_____
_____
_____
_____
_____
_____
_____
_____
_____
_____
_____

Review

Describe the law of conservation of energy:

_____

_____

_____

_____

_____

_____

What is the energy that is conserved?

    A. kinetic energy

    B. potential energy

    C. total energy

    D. chemical energy

What is usable energy?

_____

_____

Name one form of energy that is sometimes unusable.

_____

_____

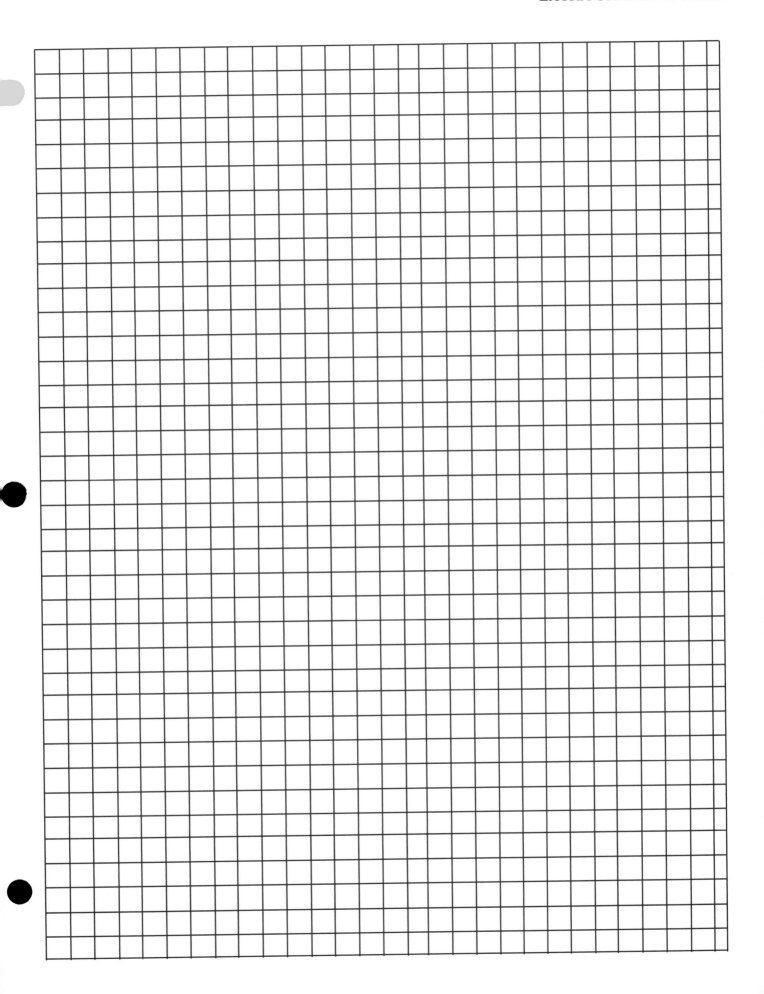

EXTRA GRAPHING PAPER